LUCKY NUMBERS!

Choose
Your Best
L**8**TTERY
Strategy

Jo Mason

D1277249

Publications International, Ltd.

Jo Mason was Texas Bureau Chief and columnist for *LottoWorld* magazine. She has written extensively about lottery, astrology, and numerology for a variety of national publications.

Copyright © 2001 Publications International, Ltd. All rights reserved. This book may not be reproduced or quoted in whole or in part by any means whatsoever without written permission from:

Louis Weber, CEO
Publications International, Ltd.
7373 North Cicero Avenue
Lincolnwood, Illinois 60712

Permission is never granted for commercial purposes.

Manufactured in U.S.A.

8 7 6 5 4 3 2 1

ISBN: 0-7853-4926-X

Contents

Introduction
Something Old, Something New, 4

Chapter 1
Games and More Games, 6

Chapter 2
Methods to the Madness, 18

Chapter 3
Numerology:
Finding Your Inner Number, 30

Chapter 4
It's All in the Timing, 41

Chapter 5
You've Got to Believe, 53

Chapter 6
Words to the Wise, 67

Something Old, Something New

○ ○ ○ ○ ○

The roots of lotteries go down deep and spread far. "Casting lots" is even mentioned in the Bible. The first lottery to offer cash prizes probably originated in Florence, Italy, in the 16th century. It was dubbed *Lotto de Firenze*, and it quickly spread to other Italian cities. The game, as well as the name, caught on. Italy's national lottery is still called Lotto, as are those in the U.S. and many other countries.

During Colonial times, lotteries were all the rage in America. Most were held for charitable or civic purposes, such as building churches, bridges, and schools. But lotteries fell into disfavor by the mid-19th century. Things changed in the second half of the 20th century. New Hampshire was the forerunner, holding its first lottery in 1964. Other states gradually followed suit. In the '80s and particularly the '90s, the ancient game became hotter than a two-dollar pistol. Today, the number of states participating in lotteries has grown to 37, plus the District of Columbia.

You'll see people of all ages and from all walks of life picking and scratching (picking numbers and scratching off instant tickets, that is). Nationwide, total annual lottery sales have grown into the billions of dollars. In most states, all it costs to take a chance on changing your life forever is $1. Where else can you buy a dream for a dollar?

Remember, no person, system, or book can truthfully guarantee to make you a lottery winner. What this book provides is a brief overview of the different games and how they're played. It gives you a slew of ideas and hot tips on what to do and what to avoid. There's even a section on what to do if you win. For the most part, it presents a host of number-picking strategies to help you overcome those long odds.

Some of these methods, such as frequency analysis, are mainstream. Some are based on ancient arts, including numerology. Still others are a tad offbeat. A few are down-right wacky.

Throughout this book, you'll find funny, heartwarming, and informative stories of real-life winners. In many of these stories, you'll read how they selected their numbers. Maybe you'll be inspired to follow in their footsteps—or develop your own unique playing style. So choose a system, have some fun, and take a chance. You just might end up a millionaire.

CHAPTER ONE

By the Numbers

New types of lottery games are popping up more and more frequently. But the basics remain Lotto, Mini Lottos (or Little Lottos), Dailies, Powerball, and Instant Games. The Instant Games are scratch-off tickets, while the other lottery games are on-line games because they consist of computer-generated tickets.

○ ○ ○ ○ ○

Let's look at the various games lottery players love to play, beginning with Lotto, which has become the most popular of all lottery games.

Lotto

In Lotto, six numbers are drawn from a range of numbers (such as 42, 44, 46, 49, 51, or 54). Michigan, for instance, has a 6-out-of-49 game (6/49), meaning that six numbers are drawn from a possible 49. Georgia's Lotto is 6/46, meaning that six numbers are drawn from a possible 46.

To play Lotto, indicate your six chosen numbers by marking the numbered squares on a play slip. Then take

the play slip to a lottery retailer (or agent). The retailer enters your selection in the on-line terminal, which produces your game ticket. The ticket, not the play slip, is the official receipt and must be presented and validated in the event of a win. Always check to make sure that the correct date and numbers are on the game ticket before you leave. Lottery agents are found in convenience stores, gas stations, and grocery stores.

The cost for one chance at Lotto is still $1 in most states. So for one chance, or play, at Lotto, you would pay $1. For five plays—that is, to play five sets of numbers—you would pay $5. Some states, such as Illinois, offer a bargain: two plays for $1.

Typically, Lotto drawings are held twice a week, usually on Wednesday and Saturday nights. However, this may not be true for every state.

The lottery officials use special ball-drawing machines, and the balls are numbered. The machine randomly shoots out six selected balls; these balls display the winning numbers for that evening's lottery drawing. If all six of your numbers exactly match the numbers drawn, you win the jackpot. In Lotto, your numbers don't need to be listed in any particular order, as long as they match those drawn. If two or more persons correctly pick the six numbers, the winners split the prize money. If no one wins, the prize

money rolls over and the jackpot becomes increasingly larger. Not surprisingly, when this occurs, more and more players take part, lured by the huge jackpot.

Now that you know how to play Lotto, you probably want to know how much you can win. The amount of the prize depends upon several factors. Lotto is a pari-mutuel game, meaning the amount of the prize is determined by the total sales for each drawing and the number of winners. Or, if there is no winner, the prize is rolled over, with an increased amount compared to the previous game. The more populous states, such as Texas, New York, and California, will usually have larger jackpots. The day after each drawing, your state lottery announces the grand prize amount for the next drawing. Even if you don't match all six numbers, you can still win a prize by matching three, four, or five of the numbers. While the payoff for matching three out of six is small, the odds are better.

Mini Lottos

Mini Lotto games have better odds and are played more often. The method of play is similar to that of Lotto, but the number of balls drawn and the playing fields are usually lower. For example, in Florida's Fantasy 5 (5/26), the player tries to correctly pick the five numbers drawn from a field of 26. In the Texas Cash 5 (5/39), you must correctly pick the five numbers drawn from a

field of 39. To play a Mini Lotto game, select five numbers from your state's field of numbers and mark your play slip. Take the play slip to a lottery agent, who will then give you your game ticket. The game is played the same way as Lotto, with the machine shooting out five selected balls instead of six. If all of your numbers exactly match the numbers drawn, you win a Mini Lotto jackpot. As in regular Lotto, your numbers do not have to be in the same order as the winning numbers.

In some states, the drawings are held more often with Mini Lotto than Lotto. They are held either three, four, or five days a week—and in some cases daily.

The amount of the prize money for Mini Lotto games works the same as Lotto. But since there are fewer "picks" (five) than in Lotto (six), your odds of winning these games are much better. You can also win smaller prize amounts if only three or four of your numbers match.

The Dailies

If you'd like to try your luck every day or are just looking for better odds, then the Pick 3 and Pick 4 might be the games for you. In most states, you can play these six or seven days a week. Thus, they are often referred to as "The Dailies."

For Pick 3 (also called Cash 3), players choose any three-digit number from 000 to 999, and for Pick 4 (or Cash

Real-Life Winner: They Shook on It

Few stories about lottery millionaires grabbed the headlines and the attention of the public more than Raul Zavaleta's. And few are as heartwarming. The McAllen, Texas, elementary physical education teacher had made an agreement with his good friend, Enrique Lozano, also a teacher. They promised each other that if either won the Lotto, they would split the prize money, no matter who bought the ticket. They shook hands to seal the pact.

One spring evening, Zavaleta's "numbers were up." He realized he held the only winning ticket to the Lotto Texas jackpot of nearly $40 million. Without hesitation, Zavaleta immediately drove to his friend's house to tell him the good news. As agreed, he split the money right down the middle with his friend, Lozano.

"There are no regrets. None," said Zavaleta. "His handshake means more to me than the money."

4), any four-digit number from 0000 to 9999. These have their own special play slips, offering several types of plays. The basic plays in most states are: exact order (straight), any order (box), exact/any (straight/box), or combination.

If you mark any order, you win if your three numbers are drawn—no matter in what order. If you choose exact/any (which, like any order, costs $1) and your three digits are in the exact order drawn, you win the prize for exact plus the

prize for any. Or if you choose the correct numbers, but not in the correct order, you still win the smaller payoff. If you mark combination, you are covering all bets. A combination play (which costs $3) gives you all possible exact (straight) combinations of your three numbers on one ticket.

Let's say for a Pick 3 game you chose the numbers 4-0-7, and the drawing results are 7-4-0. If you marked exact order, you win nothing. If you marked any order or exact/any, you win the smaller payoff. If you marked combination, you win the same amount as if you'd bought an exact (straight) ticket. Or you may have chosen the numbers 5-1-6, and the numbers drawn are 5-1-6. If you had marked any order, you would win, but not as much as if had you marked exact order or combination. And if you had purchased an exact/any ticket, you'd win even more.

Unlike Lotto, the payout on most states' daily games is not determined by the pool of players. Pick 3 and Pick 4 usually have fixed prize amounts geared to the odds. In fact, these games are associated with a different set of mathematics than Lotto. The odds in the Dailies are much lower than in Lotto, and so is the payout in case of a win. The odds of picking three digits in exact order on one play are 1,000 to one; the odds of picking four digits in exact order on one play are 10,000 to one.

Game tickets are typically 50¢ or $1, depending on the type of play selected. In the Texas Pick 3 game, if you correctly picked the three digits in the right order, and had placed 50¢ on "exact order," you'd win $250. If you had placed a $1 bet, you'd win $500.

Powerball

For those interested in *really* big stakes, there's Powerball, which has been called the closest thing the United States has to a national lottery. It's played in the District of Columbia and the following 20 states: Arizona, Connecticut, Delaware, Idaho, Indiana, Iowa, Kansas, Kentucky, Louisiana, Minnesota, Missouri, Montana, Nebraska, New Hampshire, New Mexico, Oregon, Rhode Island, South Dakota, West Virginia, and Wisconsin.

To win, the player must correctly pick five numbers drawn from a field of 49 (5/49) and also correctly pick the Powerball number, which is one number drawn from a field of 42 (1/42). Two separate ball-drawing machines are used.

Powerball has formidable odds against winning. But the payoff—sometimes exceeding $100 million—has made it one of the most popular lotteries in America. As in Lotto, you can still win a smaller amount if you correctly pick some of the numbers. These drawings are held every Wednesday and Saturday night.

Multi-State Games

States with relatively small populations have joined together and created games that have bigger jackpots. Powerball is such a game and is offered by the Multi-State Lottery Association (MUSL).

The Big Game is also played in several states: Georgia, Illinois, Maryland, Massachusetts, Michigan, New Jersey, and Virginia. Similar to Powerball, The Big Game also involves two separate drawings.

Real-Life Winner:
Good Start for a New Year

It was 5:30 A.M. on New Year's Day. Mike and Jan Broderson, however, weren't sleeping in after an evening of celebrating. Instead, Jan, an accountant, was at work at the Hy-Vee store in South Sioux City, Nebraska. That's when she discovered her store had sold a $100,000 Powerball winning ticket.

Mike was at home but already up and shaving when his wife called. "Go to the refrigerator," she said mysteriously. He did as she requested, opening the refrigerator door. "What do you want in here?" he asked. She told him to look at the December 31 Powerball tickets that were taped to the refrigerator door. When he read the numbers, she yelled, "We just won $100,000!" As for Mike, he finished shaving—but not without a few nicks.

Instant Games

The Instant Games, also called "scratch-off" games, don't involve picking numbers and may be purchased at any time. The popularity of "scratch-offs" is due to several reasons. First, the games are colorful and fun to play. Second, a player doesn't need to pick numbers or fill out a play slip. And finally, there's no waiting—just scratch off the spots.

Many states introduce new Instant Games every few weeks. Some are more popular than others and are kept going for a longer period of time. Other games are soon discontinued, only to reappear months or years later. Still others are seasonally oriented, such as the various versions of Stocking Stuffer, Holiday Cash, and Heat Wave. Different versions of the same game, such as Monopoly, Bingo, and Win for Life, sometimes crop up in several states.

With a few exceptions, the top prizes on instant tickets are much lower than Lotto jackpots. In addition to the top prizes in each game, the player has a chance to win smaller dollar amounts ranging from $1 to $50.

Here's how some of them are played: In Minnesota's Trump Card, the top possible prize is $5,000. Players scratch off the spots, and if any of their cards match the winning suit, they win the prize indicated. In Texas' Scratch Happy, players scratch off nine spots, revealing different amounts. If they get three like amounts, or two like

amounts and a Happy Face, they win that amount. Top prize in this game is $1,000.

A Scratch-Off System?

Technically speaking, there are no systems for beating these instant games. There are no numbers to pick, and the prizes are predetermined before you even buy your ticket. But "scratch" the surface of a lottery player and you'll find a system.

Some people keep tabs on the prizes already awarded in each game, and they buy only those games that have several of the larger prizes remaining. Most state lotteries have lists available that include the prize amounts of each game, how many of each there are, and how many remain.

What's New

Several states are adding new games or new twists to old games. There is a trend developing toward larger jackpots, but the odds of winning that jackpot are usually higher. However, the overall odds (of winning a smaller prize) are often lower. Powerball, for example, has gone from already stunning odds of nearly 55 million to one up to 80 million to one. But it now has nine ways to win.

California has replaced SuperLotto (18 million-to-one odds of winning the jackpot) with SuperLotto Plus (41 million to one). On the bright side, there are almost three times

as many winners in an average drawing, and the overall odds of winning have improved, from 60 to one down to 23 to one.

Recently, Lotto Texas changed from a 6/50 game to 6/54. This upped the previous jackpot odds of nearly 16 million to one to over 25 million to one.

Powerball-copycat games are becoming popular. These include Arizona's The Pick (which replaced its Lotto), Florida's Mega Money, and California's SuperLotto Plus. These are not identical, but all involve a bonus ball as in Powerball.

A Game for You

If you have not yet joined the lottery-playing crowd, but would like to, here are some questions that may help you decide which games to play: What is my style? What are my goals? What is my budget? If your style is simply playing for kicks, why not stick with the fun Instant Games? If your goal is to develop a system and make small wins on a regular basis, look into the daily games. And if your budget is tight, you might choose to stretch your playing dollar to the maximum by entering your state's Mini Lotto or Lotto.

For More Information...

You can find the drawing results for all your state or region's lottery games in your local newspaper, at any lottery retailer, or,

if you're in a hurry, on television shortly after the drawing. Other options are checking your state's Web site or calling the state hotline.

See Chapter 6 on how to find out about your state's games, rules, dates and times of drawings, and drawing results. Also, you'll discover more about their Web sites and hotlines.

Quick Picks

For the person who doesn't wish to take time to select his own numbers, Quick Picks (computer-generated random numbers) are an easy option. Instead of filling out a play slip, you simply tell the clerk you want a Quick Pick. The machine will then issue you a ticket with randomly generated numbers.

Considering the convenience of Quick Picks, why do players bother to pick their own numbers? Statistics show that 35 percent of players pick their own numbers (using a variety of methods), while 65 percent use computer-generated Quick Picks. Surprisingly, those who pick their own numbers end up with 43 percent of the jackpots, while the Quick Pick players win only 57 percent of the jackpots. Obviously, the percentages favor players who pick their own numbers.

Besides, picking your own numbers is part of the fun of lottery games. So turn the page and let the fun begin!

Methods to the Madness

The strategies you'll read about in this chapter are based on mathematics or logic. They are commonly referred to as reality-based systems. By learning such techniques as tracking, wheeling, and pooling, you may be able to improve your odds significantly.

○ ○ ○ ○ ○

Proponents of these methods are well aware of the odds they are dealing with. They know, for instance, that in Michigan's Lotto (6/49) there are 13,983,816 possible combinations for the 49 numbers. That's just another way of saying if you buy one play, the odds are 13,983,816 to one.

But the odds are much better in the Mini Lottos or the Dailies. Consequently, these "realists" often avoid the games with larger payoffs—and with similarly larger odds. When they do play the big games, these players—realizing what they're up against—do everything they possibly can to better their chances. And just what might that be? Most

lottologists (people who specialize in lottery number selection methods and strategies) and repeat winners agree that the following three methods—tracking, wheeling, and pooling—are musts for serious players.

Tracking

This popular system is often referred to as frequency analysis. In short, it involves keeping track of the individual numbers that are drawn over a period of time. You might compare it to handicapping a racehorse; rating his past performance to determine what his chances of winning are in the future.

Numbers that appear often in a certain game are called hot numbers. Some players will play these hot numbers exclusively on the assumption that since they have appeared often in the past, they should appear again in the future. But it's not as simple as that. Other players believe such numbers may be on their way out. Thus, they track the cold numbers—the overdue ones that haven't hit yet. Most experts, however, play a combination of these hot and cold numbers. Some people even play a combination of hot, cold, and personal numbers, such as birth dates.

Experts have a wide variety of opinions on tracking methods, so there's no exact formula for tracking. Once you understand the idea of frequency analysis, you can develop your own tracking formula. The winner of the very

first Lotto Texas jackpot—over $21 million—was a tracker. Janie Kallus of Schulenburg, Texas, was forced to use a rather unique method. Since there had been very few Texas numbers to track in the short history of the Texas Lotto, she tracked numbers from other states' drawings.

It's easy to find lists of previous winning numbers. Many state lotteries publish monthly newsletters with such information. Convenience stores also post lists for their customers. There are also a number of Web sites. Newspapers and specialty magazines list them as well, often including charts, diagrams, and forecasting graphs.

Wheeling

This frustrating experience may have happened to you: You buy several tickets and discover that you picked all six winning numbers; unfortunately, they weren't all on the same play. Experts claim that wheeling can help lock in all your favorite numbers and dramatically increase your odds of winning.

Wheeling isn't a system of selecting numbers, but a strategy for using all the numbers you have (however you obtained them). Wheeling consists of making up a master list of your best picks, then, using a coded system, playing them in different combinations in a sort of round-robin.

Some wheels even carry specific win guarantees. That is, if the numbers on your master list include all the winning

Real-Life Winner: Trackin' and Winnin'

Some people have more than their share of luck. Walt Chastain of Smyrna, Georgia, must be one of them. He claims to have won for 12 days in a row playing Cash 3. He says he cleared $1,000 a week in a three-month period, and so far, his take has been about $30,000.

The Georgian makes a hobby of tracking winning Cash 3 numbers. He once narrowly missed becoming a Georgia Lotto millionaire when he correctly picked five numbers out of six. "Everybody is entitled to his or her own view," says Chastain, "and if they want to think the lottery is just a game of chance, so be it." With his winnings to back him up, however, the lucky Georgian makes a strong argument for a very different opinion.

numbers—or some of them, such as four out of six—you are guaranteed to win a certain prize. None of them, of course, can guarantee you a jackpot.

As you might suspect, wheeling can involve some expense. Before beginning to wheel, first set up a budget and stick to it. Then determine how many numbers will go on your master list. You can buy your wheels from lottologists. They sell wheel blanks with various designs—grids, graphs, circles, triangles—and with different types of coding, such

as alphabetical. These wheel blanks provide various coded combinations for a number of plays; you simply fill in the blanks with your chosen numbers. Full wheels cover all possible combinations of your master-list numbers, while short wheels cover only some combinations.

You can also make the wheels yourself. If you favor certain numbers on your master list over some of the others, arrange your wheel so that those numbers are played more times. If you feel equally good about all your numbers, choose a wheel that uses each number the same amount of times. Here are two sample wheel blank systems:

Ten-Number Wheel
Master List: A B C D E F G H I J

Play #1	A	B	C	D	E	F
Play #2	A	B	F	G	H	I
Play #3	A	C	E	H	I	J
Play #4	B	C	E	F	G	H
Play #5	B	D	F	H	I	J
Play #6	C	D	F	G	I	J
Play #7	A	D	E	G	H	J

Eight-Number Wheel
Master List: A B C D E F G H

Play #1	A	B	C	E	G	H
Play #2	A	B	D	F	G	H

Play #3	B	C	D	E	F	G
Play #4	A	C	D	E	F	H

For the ten-number wheel, let's say you're playing a 6/49 Lotto, and you've chosen ten numbers you like: 2, 3, 8, 16, 18, 27, 31, 38, 40, and 44. Each of the seven lines represents one play. Now, beneath each letter, place the number from the master list that corresponds to it. Here's what the ten-number wheel will look like when you've finished:

Master List:	A	B	C	D	E	F	G	H	I	J
	2	3	8	16	18	27	31	38	40	44
Play #1	A	B	C		D		E	F		
	2	3	8		16		18	27		
Play #2	A	B				F	G	H	I	
	2	3				27	31	38	40	
Play #3	A		C		E			H	I	J
	2		8		18			38	40	44
Play #4		B	C		E	F	G	H		
		3	8		18	27	31	38		
Play #5		B		D		F		H	I	J
		3		16		27		38	40	44
Play #6			C	D		F	G		I	J
			8	16		27	31		40	44
Play #7	A			D	E		G	H		J
	2			16	18		31	38		44

Let's assume the winning numbers will be 3, 16, 18, 27, 40, and 44. As you can see, had you used this wheel and invested $7 ($1 for each play), you'd have won the following prizes:

Play #1: 4/6   Play #2: 3/6   Play #3: 3/6
Play #4: 3/6   Play #5: 5/6   Play #6: 4/6
                  Play #7: 3/6

For the eight-number wheel, let's say you're playing a 6/49 Lotto, and you've chosen eight numbers you like: 1, 6, 11, 14, 20, 21, 30, and 43. Place your lucky numbers below the letters on the master list. Each of the four lines represents one play. Now beneath each letter, place the number from the master list that corresponds to it. Here's what the eight-number wheel will look like when you're finished:

Master List:	A	B	C	D	E	F	G	H
	1	6	11	14	20	21	30	43
Play #1	A	B	C	E	G	H		
	1	6	11	20	30	43		
Play #2	A	B	D	F	G	H		
	1	6	14	21	30	43		
Play #3	B	C	D	E	F	G		
	6	11	14	20	21	30		
Play #4	A	C	D	E	F	H		
	1	11	14	20	21	43		

This time, let's assume the winning numbers will be 1, 6, 14, 20, 30, and 43. As you can see, had you used this wheel and invested $4 ($1 for each play), you'd have won the following prizes:

Play #1: 5/6   Play #3: 4/6

Play #2: 5/6   Play #4: 4/6

Special wheels are also available for the other lottery games, including the Pick 3 and Pick 4. Keep in mind that the dramatic results shown on these two wheels are *only* possible if the numbers on your master list include all the winning numbers.

Some Lotto players swear by their wheels. Marvin Foster, a businessman from Portales, New Mexico, gained the nickname "Mr. 27" because he always bought exactly $27 worth of tickets. He made frequent trips over the border to Texas (at the time, New Mexico did not yet have a lottery) to enter the Texas Lotto. These excursions proved to be very profitable for Foster. He won a $3.8 million jackpot as well as six 5-of-6 prizes, 11 4-of-6 prizes, and 12 3-of-6 prizes. That would be an impressive resume for a *town* of lottery players! What was Mr. 27's lucky method? He used 12 groups of three numbers that he selected by frequency analysis. He wheeled those numbers in various combinations.

Pooling

Pooling your money—or joining a lottery club—is a strategy for stretching your resources or getting "more bang for your buck." When you join a lottery club, you pool your money together with a number of other players, increasing the amount of tickets you can buy as well as your chances of winning. Of course, there are drawbacks. The primary drawback is that you must split any winnings with the other members. Here are some things you should know before joining a pool:

- Join only with people you trust, such as family and friends.

- If you do join a commercially run pool, make sure it is operated by trustworthy and reputable professionals.

- A private pool should have 15 members or less.

- A larger, commercially operated pool should have no more than 100 members.

- Ask for the club rules—in writing—before joining.

- Certain aspects should be clear from the beginning, such as who will keep the tickets in their possession, the exact procedure that will be followed in case of a win, and how the numbers will be obtained.

Special Software

You'll find numerous advertisements for computer software programs inside lottery-oriented publications. These can be expensive, so you'd be well advised to check out the reputation of the person or company advertising the product. They offer databases, astrology-based systems, and methods for selecting the best numbers for wheeling. Random number generators are also available; this is like having your own, personal Quick Pick machine.

More Methods

Avid lottery fans also use a host of other "scientific" methods. Here are a few:

- Odd/Even Analysis, which is where you determine the frequency of odd or even numbers.

- Pairs/Doubles Analysis, which is determining the frequency of certain numbers appearing together.

- Pick 3 and Pick 4 positions, such as in which position—first, second, or third—the digit 5 most frequently hits.

- Sector Analysis, which is tracking how frequently numbers in the low sector hit, how many in the

midrange sector hit, and how many in the higher range hit. For instance, if you're playing a 6/49 Lotto and believe the numbers will be midrange, you might choose 18, 20, 21, 23, 26, and 32.

Other, more exotic methods include using bell curves and computer algorithms to recognize number patterns. There's even a theory called the "Paint Factor." This assumes that

Real-Life Winner: A Dream Come True

Lottery winners often say they never dreamed they'd win. Not so with Alvin Wilson, a creeler at a carpet plant in Chatsworth, Georgia. He dreamed he'd win the Lotto in three weeks. But on the last day of the third week, he still hadn't won. Alvin and his wife, Barbara, who'd selected the numbers, had just bought their Lotto ticket. They were nearly home when she changed her mind about one number. Wilson immediately headed back to the store and bought Barbara's new ticket, and two extras. One ticket had a number one below Barbara's; the other had a number one above.

Barbara was miffed at him for buying the extra tickets, but it was a lucky decision: The ticket with the number one below his wife's won them $2 million.

"I still haven't grasped it yet," Wilson said.

Maybe he thinks he's still dreaming.

Real-Life Winner: Painting the Town Green?

Donald Pence of Phoenix, a self-employed house painter, was in the middle of a weekend job for one of his customers. That's when he and his wife, Shirley, learned they'd just hit the huge $101 million Powerball jackpot—one of the largest amounts ever won in the U.S.

The following day, Pence called his customer and told him he couldn't finish the job. The customer was unhappy, so Pence supplied him with the name of another painter, gave him the paint, and said there would be no charge for the work already done. Shirley, who had recently been caught in a layoff at the insurance company she worked for, said the good news couldn't have come at a better time.

The first thing the Pences did was purchase a new car for their daughter. After that, they "headed for the hills" to a town in the mountains 60 miles north of Phoenix.

the more paint covering the surface of the ball, the more slippery it is, making it more likely to slide out of the machine. An 8, for instance, will have more paint than a 1 or a 3, and double-digit numbers will have even more.

It seems that not a single mathematical, statistical, or physical aspect is overlooked when it comes to people's attempts to win Lotto!

CHAPTER THREE

Numerology: Finding Your Inner Number

Did you know that when you play your birthday numbers—as many folks do—you are using a very ancient art? This chapter delves into numerology and explains how to use your birth date to calculate your lucky numbers.

Understanding Numerology

numerology is the study of the occult meanings of numbers. Its exact origin is unknown, but it predates the time of Christ and was practiced by the Chaldeans of southern Babylonia (southern Iraq). Some believe that the mysterious design of the Pyramid of Giza was, in part, based upon numerological calculations.

When most people hear the word occult, they immediately think of witchcraft or the supernatural. Don't let the word throw you off: It merely means secret, concealed, or hidden, as in an occultation of the moon or an eclipse. So

just because subjects like astrology and numerology aren't commonly understood, don't associate them with witch-craft or the supernatural.

And in case you think those old beliefs have no bearing on today's world, think again. Why do you think archi-tects, to this day, number the floors of a tall building from 1 to 12 and then from 14 upward? And—be honest!—ask yourself: Have you ever deliberately chosen seat number 13 on an airplane?

The eminent Swiss psychiatrist, Carl Jung, who studied with Sigmund Freud and is best known for his introvert/extrovert personality classifications, devoted many writings to numerology. He stated that numbers existed before the consciousness of man existed, meaning that man discovered numbers and did not invent them. He believed that numbers play a large part in everyone's life. In Chapter 5, you'll read more about Jung's ideas.

Instead of joining the multitudes trying to decipher a predictable design or pattern in the lottery, try maximizing your chances by focusing on something far easier to pre-dict: your own personal winning pattern.

And you do have one. You may have noticed that certain numbers crop up frequently in your life, such as phone numbers, anniversaries, and addresses. Or maybe you've observed particular days or times when it seems you just can't lose—as well as those times when it seems everything

you do goes wrong! (You'll read more about this in Chapter 4.) Here's how to determine what some consider your luckiest numbers of all—your birthday numbers. In this chapter, you'll discover two different types of birthday numbers: your primary number and your secondary number. Each number is calculated in a different way.

Your Primary Number

Although some numerologists disagree as to which of the birth numbers are of greater significance, the birth date, or the primary number, is generally considered to be your most influential number. Your primary number will apply to you in every aspect from the lottery to significant anniversaries, such as births, weddings, and important career events.

Determining your primary number is a snap. It's simply the day you were born. If a person was born on December 8, 1950, his or her primary number is 8. If a person was born on a double-digit date, such as December 17, 1950, for example, the primary number is still 8; in numerology, numbers are always reduced to their lowest value: $1 + 7 = 8$.

Your Secondary Number

Another significant number in your life is your secondary number. As mentioned above, some numerologists consider it of greater importance than your primary number. Through trial and error, you can use them both, and over a period of time decide for yourself which one to use when picking your Lotto numbers.

Determining this number is only slightly more complicated than figuring your primary number. To determine your secondary number, add the numerical values of the month, day, and year of your birth together. Then reduce the total number as previously shown. The months of the year have the following values: January = 1, February = 2, March = 3, April = 4, May = 5, June = 6, July = 7, August = 8, September = 9, October = 10, November = 11, and December = 12.

The person born on December 8, 1950, will compute the secondary number like this: month + date + year. The number for December (12) reduces to 3 (1 + 2 = 3). Now add 3 (month) + 8 (day) + 1 + 9 + 5 + 0 (year); this equals 26. Then reduce the double-digit total as follows: 2 + 6 = 8. This person's secondary number is 8.

But what happens if you forget to reduce the numbers before you add them up? You'll find that no matter how you add up the numbers, and then reduce them, the result will always be the same. Using the same date, if we were to add the numbers like this—12 + 8 + 19 + 50—we'd get 89. Then we would add 8 + 9 = 17, which then reduces to 8 (1 + 7 = 8).

Other Tricks Using the Formula

The formula you just learned—adding and reducing the numbers in your birth date—may be used for determining additional lucky numbers besides your primary and secondary numbers. In fact, you can use it to obtain a single digit from any double- or triple-digit number or even from a long series of numbers.

Real-Life Winner: Numbers From Beyond

Daniel Barker of Tacoma, Washington, came to the United States from Vietnam over 25 years ago. At the time, the teenager must have realized his new country was a place of opportunity. But just what form that opportunity would take, he could never have imagined.

His deceased father appeared in a dream and gave him six numbers.

"In my dream," Barker states, "my father said this was the last time he would give me any numbers."

Obviously no high roller, he waited until an hour before the drawing, then spent only $2 in tickets. But that was all it took for Barker and his wife, Kye, to win $6 million in the Washington State Lotto. The Barkers said they would put aside some of the winnings for their three children's education. They also wanted to start an import/export business. Kye quit her job at a restaurant.

"We're still the same people," Daniel says. "The only thing different is the income."

The formula is simply to add each digit in a numerical series. Then add the digits of the sum until you've reduced it to a single digit. For example, you can calculate the numerical value of a telephone number. Let's say the number is 123-555-6789. Adding all the digits, we get $1 + 2 + 3 + 5 + 5 + 5 + 6 + 7 + 8 + 9 = 51$. Use the formula again to reduce the number: $5 + 1 = 6$. The phone number has a value of 6.

Now let's try a social security number: 111-22-3456. Adding all the digits together, we get $1 + 1 + 1 + 2 + 2 + 3 + 4 + 5 + 6 = 25$. Then reduce that to $2 + 5 = 7$. The social security number has a value of 7.

Remember, the result is always the same no matter how you add it. Instead of adding each single digit, you could add $111 + 22 + 3,456$, which equals 3,589. Now add $3 + 5 + 8 + 9$, which equals 25. Then $2 + 5 = 7$.

This process works in reverse, also. Suppose your primary number is 3, and you want to choose three lucky Pick 3 numbers. Simply choose any combination of three digits that, when added and reduced, will equal your primary number of 3. The number 408 is a good choice: $4 + 0 + 8 = 12$. This reduces to 3 ($1 + 2 = 3$). Or how about 057 for your Pick 3 numbers? Add $0 + 5 + 7 = 12$, which reduces to 3. You can use this process for choosing your Pick 4 numbers as well. If your primary number is 3, try: $1 + 0 + 6 + 5 = 12$. Reduce this to: $1 + 2 = 3$.

Real-Life Winner: An Answered Prayer

Roberto Contreras, a Cuban immigrant living in New Orleans, always kept a holy picture of St. Martin de Porres in his pocket. The retired city worker, who was living on a small pension, prayed to the saint to help him win the lottery.

It must have worked because Contreras hit a $1 million jackpot. But like St. Martin, who aided the poor and ill in Lima, Peru, Contreras wanted to help others. "It is better to give than to receive," he said.

Contreras sent thousands of dollars to Mother Teresa, the famous angel of mercy in Calcutta, and paid for a young girl's liver transplant. He continues to play the lottery because he says, "The more money I win, the more there will be to help people."

Happy Birthday

If, as numerologists believe, numbers are important in our lives, then what more significant number could you have than the day you came into existence—your birthday?

As for trying to win a Lotto jackpot with your primary number, you can play the number itself in combination with other numbers. A person born on August 15 might play her primary number, 6, with five other numbers.

You could even use several or possibly all numbers with a value of 6 when playing Lotto. As was illustrated previ-

ously, you may use any compound number that, when added and reduced, equals your primary number. Our August 15 birthday person could play 6, 15 (1 + 5 = 6), 24 (2 + 4 = 6), 33 (3 + 3 = 6), 42 (4 + 2 = 6), or 51 (5 + 1 = 6). (One thing to keep in mind when using this technique is to try to avoid popular numbers or popular series of numbers. Before playing all numbers with the same value, read the section in Chapter 6 on popular numbers.)

Another common way of using your birthday numbers is to simply list the day, month, and year. The person born on August 15, 1970, would play 8 (August), 15 (day), and 70 (year). Seventy, of course, is too high to use in most games, so you could reduce the double-digit number and play 7.

Other Nifty Numbers

Although your birth date numbers are of greatest importance—numerologically speaking—other personal numbers can also be lucky. Any significant anniversary in your life, such as a wedding, can be used. Family members' birthdays are also significant to you, since your life is most certainly intertwined with theirs.

Other personal numbers might be your age, social security number, address, phone number, and bank account number. Use your imagination, along with the tips in this book, to come up with even more significant numbers.

A couple from Ohio, both doctors, struck it rich to the tune of $8 million in the Ohio Super Lotto. Drs. Angelito Belardo and Orpha Belardo used a combination of birthdays to win.

Who says the number 13 is unlucky? Not Wendell Hobbs. He was born on the 13th and always plays number 13. Lucky Mr. Hobbs won $100,000 in the Oregon Powerball.

Californian Linda Ramos wanted to get her father a unique gift for Father's Day. She decided to use family members' special dates on the Lotto ticket she gave him. It turned out to be a truly special gift of $10 million. Her father, a retired agricultural laborer, agreed that it was the most extraordinary Father's Day present ever.

A System of the Ancients

Along with the numerology formula, there's also an ancient alphabet technique that comes to us from the Hebrew Kabala and the Chaldeans. This technique assigns numerical values to each letter of the alphabet. You can use these figures to calculate your name number. Next to the date you came into being (your birthday), what else can be more personal and significant than your name?

Numerologists and astrologers don't always agree on which alphabet number system to use (there are several), but most of them believe this is the most powerful one:

A = 1	H = 5	O = 7	V = 6
B = 2	I = 1	P = 8	W = 6
C = 3	J = 1	Q = 1	X = 5
D = 4	K = 2	R = 2	Y = 1
E = 5	L = 3	S = 3	Z = 7
F = 8	M = 4	T = 4	
G = 3	N = 5	U = 6	

To use this system, write out your name as you usually sign it. Place the corresponding number from the alphabet key shown above beneath each letter of your name. Here's how we'd get the name number of Elizabeth E. Jones:

E L I Z A B E T H   E.   J O N E S
5 3 1 7 1 2 5 4 5   5   1 7 5 5 3

Now, use the formula to add up the numbers: 5 + 3 + 1 + 7 + 1 + 2 + 5 + 4 + 5 + 5 + 1 + 7 + 5 + 5 + 3 = 59. Then reduce the total: 5 + 9 = 14. Keep reducing the total until you obtain a single digit value: 1 + 4 = 5. The name number of Elizabeth E. Jones is 5.

If Elizabeth Jones decides not to use her middle initial, she'll have a different name number.

E L I Z A B E T H   J O N E S
5 3 1 7 1 2 5 4 5   1 7 5 5 3

Adding and reducing these numbers gives us a different figure: $5 + 3 + 1 + 7 + 1 + 2 + 5 + 4 + 5 + 1 + 7 + 5 + 5 + 3 = 54$, and $5 + 4 = 9$. Thus the name number of Elizabeth Jones is 9.

But suppose she commonly goes by the name Lizzy Jones? She would have yet another name number. The name number of Lizzy Jones, using the formula above, is 4.

So what does all this mean? Certainly no one's going to suggest you change your name. But numerology—like astrology—is an esoteric art. This means that understanding your numbers is a very personal affair. While this chapter can show you how to compute various numbers, only you can decide the best way to use them.

For instance, if, like Lizzy Jones, you happen to have a nickname, you may find that the nickname number is luckier for you than your full name. So experiment with your primary and secondary numbers, and combine them with your name numbers derived from various spellings of your name. Buy a few Pick 3 tickets. You may discover that one or even two of the spellings of your name may be luckier for you than the others.

CHAPTER FOUR

It's All in the Timing

In the previous chapter, you learned how to obtain numbers derived from your birthday, from your name, and from significant people or events in your life. You also learned how to obtain lucky numbers for specific times. Now you'll discover more ways to make use of numerology. You'll read how another time-honored art, astrology, can help in your lottery playing. This chapter will aid you in formulating a plan of action made-to-order just for you.

Sun Sign Strategies

Have you ever wondered just how those predictions in newspapers and magazines are made? Astrology is based upon the theory that our daily lives are affected by the movement of the sun, moon, and planets. If you were to have a natal chart (horoscope) done, it would represent a snapshot of the heavens at your moment of birth. The astrologer then studies the chart to determine your traits and predict your future.

Since the astrologers who write for newspapers, magazines, and books have no way of determining your complete horoscope, they use the second-best method—sun signs. That is, they write sections on each of the signs, and you look up the correct sign for your birthday. Your sun sign is determined by the position of the sun when you were born. For example, if you were born between March 21 and April 19, your sign is Aries since the sun is in Aries at that time.

Sun sign astrology can't be as accurate as studying one's natal chart, but it can provide some good insight and advice for your activities, such as trying to win the lottery. Check out your sign's section for your tips.

ARIES (March 21—April 19)

Traits: impulsive, individualistic

Buy Tickets: in a skyscraper; in or near a hardware store

Best Games: Instant Games; bonus ball-type games, such as Powerball

Best Instant Games: red-colored, with words *Beat, Strike, Hot*, or *Fever*

Best Methods: use personal numbers; play a police officer's or a soldier's birthday; tracking; play hot numbers

TAURUS (April 20—May 20)

Traits: patient, stubborn

Buy Tickets: in an adobe or brick building; in a florist shop

Real-Life Winner: Money Isn't Everything

As a child in Latvia, Sam Zelikson survived the hardships of World War II, losing many relatives and both parents to the Holocaust. After immigrating to the United States, he started his own glass company. But in 1991, an event occurred that he couldn't have imagined even in his wildest dreams. He won part of New York's record-breaking $90 million jackpot (Zelikson and eight other people shared it for a total of $10 million each).

After giving his half of the company to his partner, Zelikson and his wife, Janice, bought a beautiful new home and now travel frequently. But Zelikson's early experiences taught him certain values. He reveals his philosophy: "Help the needy. Help your fellow man. Spend wisely. Most importantly, take care of your family."

Best Games: ones with large jackpots, such as Lotto or Powerball

Best Instant Games: copper-colored, with words *Treasure, Bank,* or *Vault*

Best Methods: play same series of numbers repeatedly; mainstream systems such as wheeling

GEMINI (May 21—June 21)

Traits: versatile, adaptable, restless

Buy Tickets: at a neighborhood store; in a bus or train station

Best Games: Mini-Lottos (Fantasy 5, Cash 5)

Best Instant Games: yellow-colored, with words *Fast*, *Quick*, or *Double*

Best Methods: buy two tickets; buy Quick Picks; play a sibling's birthday or your car license plate numbers

CANCER (June 22—July 22)

Traits: security-minded, moody

Buy Tickets: at a grocery store; near a river, lake, or beach

Best Games: Dailies; $2 instant games

Best Instant Games: silver-colored, with words *Money*, *Cash*, *Monopoly*, or *Millionaire*

Best Methods: make use of numerology, lucky charms, and hunches (ESP–Chapter 5)

LEO (July 23—August 22)

Traits: bold, generous, fun-loving

Buy Tickets: where kids congregate; where your sweetheart shops; in or near a sporting goods store

Best Games: Lotto; bonus ball-type games, such as Powerball

Best Instant Games: gold-colored, with words *Cat*, *Joker*, or *Gold*

Best Methods: track and play hot numbers; play a child's birthday; try a fun method from Chapter 5

VIRGO (August 23—September 22)

Traits: practical, observant

Buy Tickets: at a newsstand; in a brick building

Best Games: Little Lotto; Dailies

Best Instant Games: yellow-colored, with words *Bingo, Tree*, or *Combination*

Best Methods: tracking; pooling; play a coworker's or a doctor's birthday

LIBRA (September 23—October 23)

Traits: logical, romantic, indecisive

Buy Tickets: in a florist shop; in or near a beauty shop; where your spouse shops

Best Games: Pick 3; Lotto

Best Instant Games: copper- or pale blue-colored, with words *Sweetheart, Diamonds*, or *Two*

Best Methods: wheeling; pooling; Quick Picks; play with a partner

SCORPIO (October 24—November 21)

Traits: intense, emotional

Buy Tickets: in basement of a building; in a dimly lit place

Best Games: Lotto; instant games

Best Instant Games: red- or black-colored, with words *Life, Bonus*, or *Second Chance*

Best Methods: the paranormal (see Chapter 5); play your insurance policy numbers

SAGITTARIUS (November 22—December 21)

Traits: happy-go-lucky, impulsive

Buy Tickets: at out-of-state lotteries; near a college

Best Games: multistate games; Pick 3

Best Instant Games: purple-colored, with words *Lucky, Happy,*
  or *Triple*

Best Methods: Quick Picks; use personal numbers; play an
  in-law's birthday

CAPRICORN (December 22—January 19)

Traits: serious, practical

Buy Tickets: at a store near your job; in a wooden building

Best Games: Pick 4; Mini-Lottos

Best Instant Games: green- or brown-colored, with words
  Green, Cold, Cool, or *Tree*

Best Methods: track and play cold (overdue) numbers; use a
  lucky charm; play your boss' birth date

AQUARIUS (January 20—February 18)

Traits: intellectual, eccentric

Buy Tickets: at an airport; where your friends shop

Best Games: Lotto; Powerball, or other bonus-ball games

Best Instant Games: dark blue-colored, with words *Wild,
  Seven,* or *Surprise*

Best Methods: join a small pool; use a computer to track and
  analyze odd/even numbers

PISCES (February 19—March 20)

Traits: sensitive, emotional

Buy Tickets: at a gas station; near a lake, river, or beach

Best Games: Lotto; Mini-Lotto; Pick 3

Best Instant Games: turquoise-colored, with words *Nine,*

Fishing, or *Fantasy*
Best Methods: play numbers in your dreams; the paranormal (Chapter 5); wheeling

Timing Is Everything

In the previous chapter, you read why you should play numbers obtained from your birth date. But your natal date can also play a big part in selecting lucky times to play the lottery.

Why would you be fortunate on your birthday? The reasons are based on both astrology and numerology, which are interrelated. As far as astrology is concerned, each year the sun returns to its natal position (as it was when you were born). Astrologers call this fortuitous aspect a conjunction, and it is in effect about a week before and after your birthday. So if you were born on November 9, your luckiest lottery-playing time of the year is approximately from November 3 through November 15, with the strongest emphasis being on the birth date itself.

Joyce Scott, of Chico, California, bought a Quick Pick on her birthday. Her birthday present? She collected one-third of the $39 million California SuperLotto jackpot.

Lottery personnel and contestants had begun to joke about the "Birthday Syndrome." It seemed that in the Texas Grand Prize Drawing, seven of the $1 million winners had a birthday on or near the day of the drawing.

But your birthday is only one day out of 365. Here's how you can take advantage of those lucky vibrations with your birth date numbers at other times of the year, too. Using the formula explained in Chapter 3, you can find dates that have the same value as your primary number. For example, someone born on November 9, 1949, would have a primary number of 9. He might want to reserve a larger part of his lottery funds for the following dates of any month: the 9th, 18th (1 + 8 = 9), and 27th (2 + 7 = 9).

Or you might choose to use your secondary numbers. Someone born on June 2, 1973, would have a secondary number of 1 (6 + 2 + 1 + 9 + 7 + 3 = 28; reduce to 2 + 8 = 10; reduce to 1 + 0 = 1). She would want to make sure she played the lottery on the following dates of any month: the 1st, 10th (1 + 0 = 1), 19th (1 + 9 = 10; 1 + 0 = 1), and 28th (2 + 8 = 10; 1 + 0 = 1).

But exactly how are these dates lucky for you? Should you choose your numbers on these dates? Fill out your play slip then? Buy your ticket then? The answer to all three questions is yes.

Having already determined your primary birth number (see Chapter 3), you can now use the following chart to pinpoint some good times to play the lottery. Keep in mind that the lucky times of year listed on this chart are of secondary importance to the two-week period surrounding

Primary Number	Lucky Day of the Week	Lucky Time of the Year	Lucky Days of the Month
1	Sunday	July 23–Aug. 22	1st, 10th, 19th, 28th
2	Monday	June 22–July 22	2nd, 11th, 20th, 29th
3	Thursday	Nov. 22–Dec. 21	3rd, 12th, 21st, 30th
4	Saturday	Dec. 22–Jan. 19	4th, 13th, 22nd, 31st
5	Wednesday	May 21–June 21 Aug. 23–Sept. 22	5th, 14th, 23rd
6	Friday	April 20–May 20 Sept. 23–Oct. 23	6th, 15th, 24th
7	Wednesday	Jan. 20–Feb. 18	7th, 16th, 25th
8	Tuesday	March 21–April 19 Oct. 24–Nov. 21	8th, 17th, 26th
9	Thursday	Feb. 19–March 20	9th, 18th, 27th

your birthday. Once you've found your lucky days, why not allocate a relatively larger part of your playing funds for these special days? Doesn't it make sense to take advantage of the harmonics of the universe?

Playing by the Moon

There are other timing techniques to increase your chances of winning. Not only can you find lucky times on certain dates or months, but you also have lucky cycles that can be calculated

from hour to hour. How is this done? Just as your astrological sign is determined by the position of the sun when you were born, your lucky cycles can be determined by the position of the moon.

According to astrology, the moon governs growth. In fact, some farmers plant by the phases of the moon, checking when the moon is in a fertile or fruitful sign. Since the water signs (Pisces, Cancer, and Scorpio) are the most fertile signs for planting, a farmer would want to plant crops when the moon is in a water sign. The earth signs (Capricorn, Taurus, and Virgo) are also considered to yield a prosperous harvest. So why not follow the farmers' example and plant your lottery "seeds" (numbers) during a fruitful time?

Now, in what sign of the moon will you be luckiest? At the sign under which you were born, of course. Leos, for instance, will want to choose their numbers and buy that stack of Pick 3 tickets on the days when the moon is in Leo. The moon stays in each sign of the zodiac for approximately two and a half days. So how can you determine what sign the moon is in?

You could purchase an ephemeris, which is a complete listing of the positions of all the planets, plus the sun and the moon. Using astrology, these tables calculate the positions for past years as well as future years. Astrological

Real-Life Winner: Goblins Lend a Hand

Richard Heard of Winder, Georgia, had drawn upon a common method to pick his numbers: using his children's birth dates, ages, and other significant numbers in his life. On Halloween, he was at work on the night shift at General Motors in Doraville. Heard stopped to call a friend for the Lotto drawing results. His ticket still in his wallet, he didn't bother to check it as his friend read the numbers.

"I think four or five of them sound familiar," he said, and then returned to work.

It wasn't until his break time that he discovered that all his numbers matched, making him $1.6 million richer. Later, he realized he'd made an error on the age of his oldest son. The son was 38 instead of 36, as Richard had marked.

Some friendly goblins must have played a part in Richard's lucky mistake!

---

magazines give the moon's precise position. You can also check out some other sources for the moon's daily position, such as the farmer's almanac and some calendars. Keep in mind that if you use a calendar, your calculations may not be precise.

If your calendar lists the moon as being in Taurus for November 5, 6, and 7, you'll have no way of knowing precisely when the moon leaves Taurus and enters the sign

Real-Life Winner: She Put Something Back

Arjustice Morris, from Caldwell, Texas, usually bought a total of $10 worth of tickets a week.

"I used to have a strategy," Morris said, "but it wasn't working. So this time, I just wrote the numbers down at the last minute."

Those last-minute digits were worth over $17 million. When the numbers were announced, some of them sounded familiar, but she had to check her tickets.

"I started looking at the numbers, thinking, 'I finally got three,' then I counted four, then five, and then my husband said, 'You got them all!'"

Morris has already spent some of her winnings to build a children's community center in Caldwell. She explains, "I didn't have anything like that when I was a kid. I wanted to put something back."

of Gemini. You'll only know that it does so at some time on the seventh. You may have to use some educated guesswork, but that may be all you need to know in order to play your lucky numbers.

CHAPTER FIVE

You've Got to Believe

Do you have a taste for the paranormal, the mysterious, or even the frankly bizarre? Do you pick up pennies for luck and avoid black cats? If you've gotten this far through the book without finding a number-picking strategy, maybe you'll hit the jackpot in this chapter.

Dreaming

Of course, you can't control the things you dream about, but if you do happen to dream about a specific number, then play it. If you dream about a certain number of people or objects, play that number also. Your subconscious often gives you clues in riddles, so become adept at interpreting hints from your dreams. For instance, if you dream of buying eggs at the convenience store, play the number 12 (a dozen). Or instead, play numbers with the same value as the one you dreamed of. (Refer to the formula in Chapter 3.) For example, if you dream of the number 6, play the numbers 15, 24, 33, 42, or 51.

A Texas woman dreamed about dancing feet on three consecutive nights. Later she bought an instant Texas

Two-Step ticket that depicted a pair of cowboy boots dancing. She won over $1,000.

Even though you may not be able to control your dreams, you can keep track of them. Sleep researchers recommend this method to help you remember your dreams: Keep paper and pencil within reach of your bed. Before you fall asleep, tell yourself that you will remember your dreams. When you wake up in the morning, try to recall the night's dreams while they're still fresh in your mind. Think about your dreams, and then write down as much as you can remember before you forget. And definitely jot down any numbers you see in your dreams.

ESP

Contrary to popular opinion, extrasensory perception (ESP) is not the exclusive property of seers. Chances are you have it—to some degree. For instance, the phone rings, and you know who's calling before you even pick it up—and you don't have caller ID. There are several types of ESP.

Telepathy is the ability to send or receive thoughts from others without using any of the five senses. It's commonly called mind-reading. Even if you have telepathic power, it isn't likely to win you a jackpot. Why? Because no one knows what those numbers will be before the drawing; therefore, there is no information to be sent or to receive.

Real-Life Winner: Patience Pays

A woman with an unusual name, Melvin Miller, had an even more unusual dream. Six numbers—4, 19, 21, 27, 31, and 37—appeared to her. The Washington Park, Illinois, resident was sure the dream was a message from God, and someday she'd win the lottery. So she patiently played those six numbers over and over.

One day, Miller was driving around an expensive neighborhood, and she fell in love with a home being built. (The price tag was $300,000.) To the amusement of the construction workers, she stopped her car, got out, and loudly proclaimed the house hers.

Ten years later, her persistence paid off when she became a $22 million prize winner. Then what? She purchased the $300,000 dream home, of course!

Clairvoyance is the ability to perceive objects or events in the past, present, or future without using any of the five senses. It's commonly called "seeing the future." And yes, if you are one of the few who possess clairvoyance, it could help you win the lottery.

Some unique individuals' extrasensory powers operate more or less at a high level throughout their lifetimes. They are known as sensitives, mentalists, seers, or psychics. Most of us, however, are limited to an occasional flash of

intuition. So if you ever have a hunch that you should play a certain number or series of numbers, just do it.

More than one person has had a feeling he should play the lottery and later has been glad he did. Richard Jacobs of Mirimar, Florida, had played the Lotto only once before, but he "had a hunch" that he should play again. He ended up with over $4 million.

Some Hot Tips for the Calendar Year

JANUARY: Play the digit 1 since the first day of the year is in January and it's the first month of the year. Play the number of New Year's resolutions you made.

FEBRUARY: On Valentine's Day, play your sweetheart's birthday or the numbers 2 and 14. If it's a leap year, use the number 29. Play the birth dates of Washington and Lincoln.

MARCH: Wear green and play the numbers 3 and 17 on St. Patrick's Day. Buy an extra ticket if you're Irish. Play the date of the vernal equinox (the first day of spring).

APRIL: Time to "spring forward" with daylight saving time. Go one up on the numbers you've been playing. Example: If you've been playing 5, 19, 21, 22, 36, and 47, play 6, 20, 22, 23, 37, and 48 instead.

MAY: Play your mom's birthday, age, phone number, or address on Mother's Day. On Memorial Day, play birthdays of deceased relatives or deceased veterans.

JUNE: On Flag Day, play the numbers 6 and 14. Or play 13, the number of stars on the original American flag. Use your favorite graduate's birthday, age, or grade point average. On Father's Day, play Dad's birth date.

JULY: Play the numbers 7 and 4 on Independence Day. Play 56 (or reduce it using the formula) for the 56 people who signed our Declaration of Independence.

AUGUST: There are no holidays in August, but the dog days of summer come to an end. Play your pet dog's birth date if you know it. If not, use the numbers on his tags. Watch the Perseid meteor showers; use the number of shooting stars you see.

SEPTEMBER: Play the date of Labor Day and the date of the autumnal equinox (the first day of fall). Do you have a child or grandchild attending school? Play the grade he or she will be in.

OCTOBER: When daylight saving time ends, we "fall back." So subtract a digit from each number: If you've picked 3, 18, 19, 24, 30, and 49, play 2, 17, 18, 23, 29, and 48 instead. On Halloween, count how many little goblins come to your door.

NOVEMBER: On Thanksgiving Day, use the number of pounds your turkey weighs. On Election Day, play the number of votes your favorite candidate received. (You can always reduce a large number.)

DECEMBER: Play the numbers 12, 24, and 25 all month. After Christmas, play the number of greeting cards you sent or received. Use the date of the first day of winter as well.

Lucky Charms and More

Charms, amulets, and talismans are supposed to have magical powers. Traditionally, they are carried on one's person, or around one's neck, or the object is touched in some way in order for it to work. This touching of the lucky object is a belief in many cultures. In Mexico and other Latin American countries, you must touch a person or item that you verbally admire or risk invoking *El Ojo*, the Evil Eye. For instance, don't tell a woman in a grocery store that her baby is cute unless you give the child a small pat or tweak his toe.

American Indian lore is filled with charmed objects, such as the Navajo mandalas—which are amulets composed of feathers, leather, and fur—and the shamanic or totem animals.

Traditional folklore includes some common charms you've probably seen or used before, such as an old copper penny, a silver coin, a four-leaf clover, a rabbit's foot, or a horseshoe. Even another person can be a lucky charm. Does a lucky charm really work? Who knows? But there are some people who are glad they believe in lucky charms.

Andy Bownnleur's experience shows that there is such a thing as "the magic touch." The Virginia resident rubbed the shoulders of a friend who'd already won the Lotto and then became a $2 million winner himself.

A car turned out to be a lucky charm for Johnny and Becky Taylor. They bought a GMC van that had been previously owned by a Florida Lotto winner. Now they themselves are $7.9 million Lotto winners, and they give credit to the car for their good fortune.

Divination

This is the art of foretelling the future by means of auguries, signs, and omens. In ancient times, soothsayers inspected animal bones and entrails to make predictions. This was called haruspication. Ancient Greeks threw wine into a basin and then observed the splash pattern. This was called kottabos. Polynesians would spin a coconut or niu to determine one's fate. And ancient Romans used knucklebones or astragali, which are similar to our dice.

What are some methods you might try (in case you dislike wasting good wine or are fresh out of entrails)? Create your own divination techniques. You could toss a coin, throw dice, pick cards from a deck of playing cards, or try bibliomancy. This is the system of using a favorite book or the Bible to pick your numbers. You open the book or the

Bible to any page and then use numbers found on that page. Who knows? You may end up as blessed as Bernie Bobowicz of Clifton, New Jersey. He was going through his mother's old Bible and saw some numbers. Then he got a funny feeling—a voice inside telling him to play those numbers. He won $7 million in the New York Lotto.

Praying

Not everyone would think it appropriate to appeal to the deity for something as mercenary as winning the lottery. Then again, maybe you feel you have a special use for the money. When it comes to the long odds of beating the lottery, you can certainly use a little help from high places.

A parish priest, Father Roberto Russo, of London, England, has won over 30,000 pounds, two cars, and three vacations over the last 20 years in raffles. He donates most of what he wins to charities but confesses he does permit himself one glass of wine a day from the bottles he won. One of his parishioners gives him five pounds a week to play for him in the lottery, sure that the good Father can win a bundle for him.

Superstitions

Many people today consider these old superstitions quaint. Some had their beginnings in ancient religions or the occult

arts. Others were based on logic, according to what was then believed as fact. For instance, your reflection was considered part of your soul; thus breaking a mirror would be a disaster. Other beliefs originate in the folklore of different lands. The origins of still others have become lost in the dim past. Here are some common and not-so-common superstitions to keep in mind the next time you pick your lottery numbers:

- Knock on wood as you select those numbers. The Druids believed that spirits dwelt inside of trees, so they knocked on wood to summon the spirits.

- Cross your fingers for luck. This was most likely derived from the Christian cross.

- Wear red clothing when you buy your ticket. In Chinese folklore, the color red (along with loud noises) frightens evil spirits away.

- Never play all odd numbers on one play. Chinese custom says the world is ruled by two principles, Yin and Yang. Odd numbers are Yang and belong to the gods, while even numbers are Yin and belong to humans. If you select all odd numbers, you would anger the gods.

Shawnda Kilpatrick, a student at Howard University in Washington, D.C., was temporarily working in her

hometown of Houston. She was one of the eight lucky winners of the Win for Life instant game that pays $1,000 a week for life. She says her mother had made her and her brothers put black-eyed peas in their pockets on New Year's Day.

Off-the-Wall Ways

- When you fill your car with gas, check out the numbers—price and gallons—on the pump. Use those digits on the ticket you buy at the gas station.

- While filling out the play slip, look at the clock and play the current time.

- If you take your temperature or take your blood pressure, play those numbers.

- Try the jersey numbers of your favorite athletes.

- If there's a blue moon (a second full moon in a month), buy an extra ticket. Everyone deserves to win once in a blue moon!

- Play the address of the lottery retailer.

- Brides are considered lucky. If you attend a wedding, ask the bride to pick some numbers for you.

Real-Life Winner:
What a Difference a Digit Makes

There have been many reports of players who used the same series of numbers for years before finally winning the jackpot. In the case of Shirley Peters of Fruitland Park, Florida, her story has a bit of a twist to it: In her words, "It was a fluke." Peters, a beauty shop owner, played the same set of numbers in the Florida Lotto for 12 years. Then, in April 2000, she decided on a whim to change just one number: Instead of 39, she played 30. That was all it took to match the six winning numbers. She walked away with a single Cash Option prize of $1.5 million.

Peters, though, said she had no plans to retire. In fact, she planned to buy a new beauty shop. It looks as though her wave of good luck may just be permanent.

- Use a Chinese version of Quick Picks—play fortune cookie numbers.

- Try your license plate or vehicle ID numbers.

- If you become stuck in a traffic jam, play the numbers on the license plate of the vehicle ahead of you.

- If you're the parent or grandparent of twins, play numbers with the value of two.

- Horse racing fan? Use your favorite horse's race number, prerace odds, starting position number, or finish position. If he wins, places, or shows, play the payoff amount.

- Wear your birthstone while picking numbers and buying lottery tickets. Rub the gem for luck. This is an especially lucky thing to do on your birthday.

James Herbert of Matteson, Illinois, was driving along, minding his own business, when a big truck nearly sideswiped him and almost ran him off the road. He copied down the license plate numbers along with other numbers on the truck and later played them in the Lotto. They were a big "hit"—$2.8 million worth.

A sign painter from Vidor, Texas, Oliver Dooley decided to try a new method. He took his nonwinning lottery tickets, cut the numbers out, and put them in a coffee cup. He stirred them, drew six pieces of paper, and played the numbers he picked. Dooley's innovative method won him $6.4 million.

Darlene Sharp of Havre, Montana, owes her huge $47 million win to her herd of cattle. She used their ear-tag numbers in combination with the number of heifers and steers she owned on her lottery play slip.

The Unexplained

In Chapter 3 you read about Carl Jung and his interest in numbers. He also made a lifetime study of coincidence. Jung attributed these occurrences to unknown forces seeking to bring order to a chaotic world. In 1952 he wrote that coincidences happen more frequently than probability theories would predict. He called the phenomenon synchronicity—when seemingly unrelated events occur in some unexpected association with each other. Certainly, when it comes to lottery games, some very strange things indeed have occurred. As to whether they are random occurrences or synchronicity, pure chance or fate, only you can decide.

Fred Thompson of North Haven, Connecticut, had played 111 in the Pick 3 Game for days with no luck. But when he went to the store, he bought a Lotto ticket on a whim and forgot his usual Pick 3. That night he watched in dismay as the winning Pick 3 numbers—111—were announced. He wasn't disappointed for long, though. Shortly afterward, he found his Lotto ticket had won him $3.2 million.

Remember Bernie Bobowicz, who won the New York Lotto? Several years before he found the six winning numbers in the Bible, he had won over $3 million using his old army dog-tag numbers. And on the day he won using the Bible, he also picked five of six on another ticket.

In July 2000, Lotto Texas changed its field of numbers from 50 to 54. On the very first night, the six numbers drawn were 9, 28, 35, 51, 53, and 54. In a seemingly incredible coincidence, three of the four new numbers were drawn. Some people were skeptical, believing the drawing results were too coincidental. "It's rare, but not that rare," states Keith Baggerly, an assistant professor of statistics at Rice University. He says the odds were 1 in 330 that three of the new balls would be drawn.

Synchronicity and You

If Jung's theory appeals to you, then your challenge is this: Assimilate what you read in this book about traditional methods, numerology, astrology, dreams, charms, and so forth. Then use all those ideas creatively in connection with people and things that are personally significant to you, such as your family members, house, job, and hobbies.

Reread some of the examples, and see if they tie in with what you've learned. Who's to say that the people who used a toy spinner to win $14 million weren't actually making use of the ancient art of divination?

CHAPTER SIX

Words to the Wise

You've read about the different lottery games and how to play them. You've also found several methods of picking lucky numbers. Now it's time to fine-tune your game using this chapter full of insider tips and techniques. Know what to do and what to avoid. Learn how to set up a lottery-playing budget. Discover different ways to get in touch with your state's lottery. Finally (may the odds be with you), know what to do if you win!

Prudent Precautions

I f possible, always buy your own lottery tickets. Don't ask neighbors or friends to pick them up for you. Similarly, don't pick up tickets for others. Don't loan or borrow money for tickets, and don't go halfsies, either. Why? Isn't this a trifling matter—the same as picking up a loaf of bread for someone at the store? Not quite. If the ticket doesn't win or if the prize is small, then there's usually no problem. But if the ticket turns out

to be a jackpot winner, you could have a sticky situation on your hands. At the very least, it could be embarrassing. This little favor for a neighbor now involves millions of dollars.

For instance, maybe your neighbor said she'd pay you the dollar for the ticket later. Fine, you think. What's a dollar? You give her the ticket, and she's now a millionaire. Be honest. Would you perhaps feel you're entitled to part of the windfall? After all, you did buy the ticket with your own money. OK, it wasn't technically your money. It was money you loaned your neighbor. Still, you did go and purchase the ticket, so you might feel you're entitled to some of the winnings.

What if the situation were reversed, and your neighbor had purchased the ticket for you? Maybe you jokingly promised to split the money with her if you won. Are you aware she could take you to court, claiming the two of you made a verbal agreement? No matter what people's good intentions are before the ticket is purchased, not everyone is as honorable as Raul Zavaleta, one of the real-life winners featured in this book. Once the winning numbers are announced, not everyone will, without hesitation, keep his or her promise to split $40 million.

Are you beginning to see the possible repercussions in this? Why not avoid broken friendships, hurt feelings, and even lawsuits? Buy your own tickets, period. It's an entirely

different situation when you give a ticket to someone as a gift, or vice versa—a gift is a gift.

Most people discard their losing scratch-off, Pick 3, and Lotto tickets. After all, what possible use could you have for those scraps of paper? Think again. If you regularly spend a significant amount of money on the lottery, those old tickets might be worth cash to you.

The IRS says you cannot offset losses against winnings and report the difference. For example, if Mary spends $500 a year on the Pick 3 game and wins only $40, she must report the $40 even though her losses amounted to $460. According to the tax rules, if you have gambling losses, you can claim them as an itemized deduction, but you cannot deduct more than the winnings reported. So if Mary itemizes her deductions, she can take only $40 as an itemized loss on schedule A.

On the other hand, if Jim spends $200 and wins $500, he too must report the $500. But if he itemizes, he can claim the entire $200 as a loss on schedule A since he is allowed to report any losses up to $500. Ironically, this law helps winners more than it helps losers. So think positively. Think like a winner, and save those old tickets.

In case you live in one of the states that doesn't have a lottery, you may be tempted to enter lotteries in other states. That's fine, provided you go to the area and purchase

the ticket in person. There are several federal and state laws concerning the lotteries. One is the U.S. Postal Service regulation that forbids the mailing of lottery tickets.

Some firms, for a fee, sell receipts that allow you to take part in other lotteries. If your state has a lottery, it makes little sense to enter either out-of-state or foreign lotteries. Chances are you'll find better odds right in your own backyard, without the extra fee or the risk. Can you imagine winning several million dollars only to discover that you haven't actually won it after all?

It seems that any time big money is involved, there are those who try to get a piece of the action—illegally. You'll frequently see ads in magazines and newspapers for books, software, and other media to help you in your goal to win the Lotto. Many of these are reputable businesses and can offer you professionally designed wheeling systems and other strategies that may help better your chances. But if one of these companies claims their product is guaranteed to make you the next Lotto millionaire, ask yourself one very obvious question: If they've managed to solve the riddle of how to win a jackpot, why are they running an ad?

Playing Smart

If you've been playing for any length of time, by now you've surely heard the advice: "Don't play popular numbers." Why?

Certain groups or combinations of numbers are played by hundreds or even thousands of people on any one Lotto night. So why would you care about that? Because if you played 1, 2, 3, 4, 5, and 6 and those numbers were drawn, there may be thousands of people to split the prize with. In a $5 million jackpot, you could end up with less than a Pick 3 payoff. What are the popular combinations? There are the sequences such as the one just given as well as sequences of multiples of a certain number. One popular sequence, which consists of multiples of the number 5, is 5, 10, 15, 20, 25, and 30. And because the number is considered lucky, people often play the multiples of 7: 14, 21, 28, 35, 42, and 49.

Another less common practice is to use all numbers of the same value. Sometimes people will play all numbers with the value of the number 3: 3, 12, 21, 30, 39, and 48. Suppose your primary number (refer to Chapter 3) is 3, because your birthday is March 21. As you previously learned, 21—or any number with the value of 3—is lucky for you. However, don't use them all on the same play slip. Spread them out over several different plays.

Other selections aren't so apparent. What, you might ask, is so common about this combination: 8, 11, 18, 21, 28, and 31? If you fill in these squares on most states' Lotto play slips, you'll see that these make a zigzag pattern. Many people select numbers that, when marked in

the squares, create a design on the play slip. Common patterns are horizontal, vertical, and diagonal lines; letters of the alphabet such as X or M; the four corners and center of the play slip; zigzags; and crosses.

Even if you do win, playing popular ticket patterns will reduce your share of the jackpot—sometimes significantly. The typical five-out-of-five pot for a Florida Fantasy 5 drawing is approximately $20,000. On June 16, 2000, the payoff for winners who picked five out of five correctly was just a little over $1,500. Why? The winning numbers—3, 11, 13, 15, and 23—formed a perfect cross. People tend to think alike when it comes to playing numbers, so try to avoid the most logical patterns of play.

As for the most popular single numbers (those not part of a popular series), they are 1 through 31—the birthday numbers. This is not to say you should avoid playing your birth date. (As you learned in Chapter 3, it is a very lucky number for you.) Just don't make a habit of playing all low numbers on one ticket. Keep in mind that the digits 1 through 9 are even more popular. Keep those to a minimum.

It seems there are few hard and fast rules in Lotto, though. There have been multimillion-dollar jackpots in which the winning numbers were all low ones (but since they weren't popular combinations of low numbers, the winners didn't have to split the jackpot with many other winners).

Although the results aren't as dramatically disappointing as with popular numbers, another way you may lose out—even if you win—is when the jackpot is large. When there is no winner for a while, the prize money rolls over and, in a sort of snowball effect, grows ever larger. The more people buy tickets, the bigger the jackpot grows. And the bigger it grows, the more people buy tickets. Lured by pots of $30 million, $50 million, and higher, players come out of the woodwork. Even those who don't usually play the lottery will play the lottery! So if you correctly pick five out of six, there will be many more five-out-of-six winners than usual—and less money for you.

If the name of the game is to win, and the way to win is to lessen the odds, why join the crowd? Go ahead and buy a ticket for the big-money drawing. But smart players quietly prefer the "small" jackpots, those of only $2 million, $4.5 million, or $6 million. This is called maximizing the value of your prize. If you think about it, those "small" jackpots would be pretty nice prizes to win, too.

Make a Budget

There seems to be nearly as many budgets for lottery play as there are playing strategies. Some believe "when you're hot, you're hot," and when you're on a winning streak, you should continue to bet. You'll be inclined to agree with that, especially

if you read Chapter 4, with its theory that some time periods in our lives are more lucky than others.

But too many people go about it the wrong way. For example, you may buy $8 worth of scratch-off tickets one morning and win $20 and $5. Not bad, you think. So you then put $5 on the Pick 3 game, purchasing $5 worth. You end up winning $40. Then you decide to place the $25 you got from the instant tickets on the Powerball. You don't win anything on the Powerball.

So, how did you do? You originally spent $8 on the scratch-off tickets. So before you entered the Pick 3, you were $17 ahead. You spent $5 on the Pick 3, so before you entered Powerball, you were $52 ahead. So far, so good. After playing Powerball, you are exactly $27 ahead. After all that excitement, it seems like a letdown, right? Of course, you can always say, "Well, I did come out ahead."

Here's what you should have done. You were right in assuming you were on a roll, and you were right to take advantage of it. But instead of placing $25 on Powerball, you should have put only $5 on the game. Then you would still be $47 on the plus side.

The mistake you made was a common one: placing the "$25 you won on the scratch-off tickets" on Powerball. The truth is, you didn't win $25 on the instant tickets. Since you had to spend $8 to buy them, you won only $17.

Sometimes we have a knack for conveniently forgetting our original investments. Next time, reinvest only the amount you began with or less. In this case, that would have been $8 or less.

The best thing to do is to draw up a plan in which you spend a certain amount per month. Be consistent. Never, for any reason, go over this amount. When you're on a roll, reinvest only the amount you started with. Set aside your regular amount for next month's playing, and put the rest of your profits in the bank, in a drawer, or in a shoe. This idea is used by players in the stock markets and other money markets and is a simple one: Let your profits ride, and cut your losses. Remember that rule whenever you play the lottery, and you'll enjoy the games much more.

Getting in Touch With the Lotteries

As you read earlier, there are several ways of finding out about the lottery. Sometimes, however, you'll need to contact the lottery itself, either directly or indirectly, for answers to your questions. The different states vary as to which medium gives what information. Here's what you can expect to find—and where:

- **Newsletters**—Again, each state differs as to information given. But generally, the publications (you'll find them free at lottery retailers) contain at least some of the following: new games (on-line and instant), prizes

remaining on instant games, special promotions, brief winner stories, winning numbers for the past weeks or months, and hot/cold numbers.

• **Hotlines**—Find these in the phone book, at the retailers, or on the Web site. A few are toll-free, but most are not. Most feature a series of recorded messages, which you select by pressing certain buttons on your Touch-Tone phone. You may be able to speak to someone in person if you wish. You may learn the current jackpot amount, whether anyone won the latest jackpot, the payoff for the on-line games, some of the new promotions or instant games and how they're played, how to claim your prize, and more. Drawing results may or may not be given here.

• **Web Sites**—These are now the preferred method to learn about your state's lottery. They generally offer a gold mine of information. Variously, you may discover the legal age to play, games (existing and upcoming), instant games (some with graphics), odds, playing instructions, times and dates of drawings, and drawing results (some extending several months into the past). You may also read about new winners and learn how to collect your prize money. Some sites offer a Frequently Asked Questions section.

Real-Life Winners: Just Call Us Rich

Richard Castellone and Richard Bleakely had been pals since early childhood. The two close friends, both from Westchester County, New York, agreed that if either won the lottery, they'd share the money.

Castellone and his wife have four children, while Bleakely and his wife have three. One evening the adults allowed the kids to use a toy spinner to pick the lottery numbers. The next day while reading the newspaper, Bleakely discovered that their numbers matched for the New York jackpot. He spent the day confirming that the numbers were indeed the right ones and that there was but one winning ticket—his and Castellone's.

Meanwhile, Castellone was at work and hadn't the slightest idea he was now a millionaire. He was over-joyed when he heard the news from Bleakely. The two buddies have shared a lot over the years. Now they'll share equal parts of $14 million!

- **E-mail**—Have questions? E-mail them to your state lottery. You'll find the address on the Web site.

- **Lottery Claim Centers or Headquarters**—These will be discussed in the section on what to do if you win.

You can reach the Web site (usually listed in the newsletter or over the hotline) directly. Another way is to check the Web

site (www.naspl.org) of North American Association of State & Provincial Lotteries (NASPL). This has links to all the North American lotteries. Or check out www.musl.com to find out more about Powerball and other games offered by the Multi-State Lottery Association (discussed in Chapter 1).

If You Win

Before you can win, you must first find out if you hold a winning ticket. Always double-check the date and the numbers on your lottery tickets with the winning numbers for that day's drawing. And if you missed the drawing on television, it's also a good idea to check more than one source. The Michigan Lotto hotline once gave the wrong winning numbers for the Daily 4. The mistake was corrected in a few minutes, but can you imagine the dismay of anyone who destroyed his ticket and later found out he'd won? And it wouldn't hurt to give that scratch-off ticket another glance before you throw it away just to make sure you haven't beaten the dealer, opened the cash vault, spun 'n' won, bingoed, won for life, or otherwise come into some cash.

Incredible as it may seem, literally millions of dollars go unclaimed each year. For whatever reasons, people may get rid of a ticket, lose it, or throw it away by mistake. But their loss can become someone else's gain.

Here is some important information for lucky winners:

• First and foremost: Whether you've won a little or a lot—even before you're sure you have won—sign the ticket. Unsigned, the ticket is a bearer instrument. This means it belongs to the bearer just like cash.

• Don't let time run out. Many states' deadlines for on-line games are 180 days from the date of the drawing. But time limits vary from state to state and from game to game, so check the previously mentioned sources, the back of the play slip, or the back of the instant ticket to make sure.

• Some states have different rules, but generally you can take your winning ticket that's less than $600 to the lottery retailer, who will pay you the money.

• Again, generally speaking, winning tickets that are $600 or over (but usually not jackpot tickets) may be cashed by taking the ticket to a state claim center. There you'll fill out a claim form and collect your prize. You can find claim center phone numbers or addresses in the phone book or at the retailers.

• In the case of jackpots, some states pay in one lump sum. Others pay by annuity (installments over a period

of years). Still others give you a choice. Sometimes this choice must be made when you buy the ticket.

- Be aware that 28 percent in federal taxes will be taken off the top before you receive your prize.

- Important: See a tax attorney before collecting the prize. If a jackpot winner dies, heirs will get the money just as any other holding, such as real estate. But unless the deceased has set up legal trusts, inheritance taxes could wipe out nearly the entire fortune.

- If you win "the big one," as stated earlier, sign the ticket. Keep it in a safe place. Verify that you are indeed the winner. See an attorney. Then contact your state lottery headquarters, who will arrange for a day for you to come in, have your ticket validated, and collect your prize money.

- Keep a low profile. Aside from the lawyer and close family members, tell no one. Until you've had your ticket validated, you're in a somewhat precarious situation. For your own safety—not to mention that of the ticket—the fewer who know, the better.

- Finally, wear a pair of sunglasses to keep the limelight out of your eyes. Wear a smile for the cameras. You're a winner. Congratulations!